*Chad Mansbridge illuminates the Cross as the great divide in human history. His book is intelligent, challenging, and important. Read it and experience the freedom of God's grace like never before.*

**Dr. Andrew Farley—Bestselling Author,**
**God Without Religion and The Naked Gospel, USA**

*This book is a great blessing! You will be astonished by God's amazing grace for every believer as it builds your faith in His unconditional love and blessings for His children. All the blessings in your life have only one source: Jesus Christ our Lord, Saviour, and Shepherd.*

**Peter Paauwe—Lead Pastor,**
**DoorBrekers Church, Netherlands**

*What has so blessed me as I have read through this book is to witness how Chad is able to marry profound and deep truths with such a precious simplicity. In over fifty years of ministry, I have never seen these tremendously deep doctrines presented in such an easy-to-understand manner. If we were to somehow get a copy of this book into the hands of every Christian leader, and were they to truly grasp the revelation of the wonder of the New Covenant, we would witness Christianity as Christ intended it, and as Paul portrayed it to be.*

**Peter Vacca—Apostle & Founder,**
**Bethesda Ministries International, Australia**

*This book is equipping believers around the world to be released into their full identity in Christ. He Qualifies You! provides vital keys to understanding the covenant we are now under, and will bring you greater levels of freedom and confidence to walk out your God-given destiny. In these pages Chad Mansbridge reveals convincingly that because of the price Jesus has paid, each one of us is fully qualified to release the Kingdom of God in power and bring the realities of Heaven to earth.*

**Chris Gore—Director of Healing Ministries, Bethel Church,**
**Redding, California, USA**

*Simply*

*It is impossible to be an effective, true-to-the-Bible Jesus follower without reaching one's own convictions on this majestic subject. Chad has provided a most outstanding outline for every believer to explore their faith around. It is not just a read. It is a journey of revelation.*

**Chris Wienand—Movemental Motivator,**
**California, USA**

*In this outstanding book, Chad Mansbridge does in less than 100 pages what most authors struggle to accomplish in two or three times that many! With clarity, precision, and joyful exuberance, Chad reveals to us God's view of mankind—full of love and grace. As the leader of a church planting movement, I couldn't ask for a better book to put in the hands of both new believers and church leaders themselves.*

**Lucas Miles—Founder & President,**
**Oasis Network for Churches, Indiana, USA**

*I love that the littlest books can announce the greatest truths! In the covenant of all eternity—the one between God and His Son, Jesus Christ—we see the power of Love at Their best, closure to ritual, and the birth of sonship. In the most disarming way, Chad invites us to sit amicably around the wedding table of the Lamb; to receive like children what we cannot work for, in order to partake in all that He worked for, like mature sons. This read is our eternal resumé!*

**Isi de Gersigny—Prophetic Psalmist & Songwriter,**
**Songs for the Nations, Sydney, Australia**

*In my opinion, Chad Mansbridge has written a masterpiece that is a critical piece in revealing the true gospel that God is once again unveiling across the world today. I have never read a piece so clear and revelational on how the three major covenants relate to Christians today. I would recommend this book to anyone who has any confusion about how the law covenant is completely obsolete, and especially to those who are struggling to grasp grace. This book clears it all up and releases a wonderful joy that comes with the discovery of the truth.*

**Ryan Rufus—Founder & Director,**
**New Nature Ministries, Australia**

Believe ✳

# He Qualifies You!

## You!

Inheriting the *Blessing* through the Gospel of Grace

Chad M. Mansbridge

**HE QUALIFIES YOU!**

**INHERITING THE BLESSING THROUGH THE GOSPEL OF GRACE**

**© CHAD M. MANSBRIDGE 2010**

**WWW.CHADMANSBRIDGE.COM**

First Edition published by New Nature Publications (2010)

Second Edition published by Seraph Creative (2017)

Third Edition published by Living Letters Publishing (2021)

Typesetting and layout by FelineGraphics : www.felinegraphics.com

Published by Living Letters Publishing : www.livingletterspublishing.com

ISBN 978-0-9953862-7-3 (Paperback)

*Dad… ultimately this book, and whatever fruit that may come as a result of people reading it, is for You Alone. I love and admire You more than words can express or time will allow. Yet another reason I am grateful to You for the promise of Eternal Life through Jesus. Thanks for everything.*

*To Jaye and our kids… I love you guys so much. Thanks for journeying with me through all the fun and all the challenges. Remember, He's worth it.*

*To Bayside, our local church family… serving and sharing our lives with you has been our great honour and privilege. You see the best and the worst in us yet love us the same. What more could we ask?*

*Rob & Glenda… you have influenced and helped shape us more than you know. I am more than happy to help keep your bookcase in place.*

*Mum & Dad… you know I am expecting a Mars Bar for this.* ☺

*Finally, to all our friends and family in life and ministry across the globe, too many to be named or numbered… give all you can to know Him, and to make Him known to others. In some small but significant way, I trust this book helps towards that end.*

And pray for us, too, that God may open a door for our message, so that we may proclaim the mystery of Christ, for which I am in chains. **Pray that I may proclaim it clearly**, as I should.

Colossians 4:3–4

Pray also for me, that whenever I open my mouth, words may be given me so that I will fearlessly make known the mystery of the gospel, for which I am an ambassador in chains. **Pray that I may declare it fearlessly**, as I should.

Ephesians 6:19–20

# CONTENTS

# FOREWORD

In all my years of Christian life and ministry, I have never read a book that imparts such clarity to a subject in which so much ambiguity abounds!

As sons of God, our common enemy has taken advantage of the confusion caused by both intentional and ignorant blurring of the Three Covenants. As a result of this inter-covenant breeding, many Christians 'having begun with the Spirit', have now embraced a distorted gospel... drinking a crippling cocktail of law and grace.

In response to this, a Grace Revolution is rapidly spreading across the earth! It is being characterised by a pure biblical theology that rightly divides the Word of Truth, restoring the life, love, and liberty of the Gospel back to the people of God!

In this book, Chad Mansbridge has distinguished himself by bringing out the distilled essence of covenant truth that shines like a jewelled diamond, revealed as brilliant and beautiful because of the art of profound succinctness and simplicity.

This presentation is precisely what is needed to precipitate perfect peace for those who have been ambushed by ambiguity, scarred by schizophrenic religion, and blurred or bullied out of their inheritance.

God is not the author of confusion.

Chad burst into my life in 1997 like a breath of fresh air. Behind his youthful enthusiasm and hunger for truth, I discerned a pure heart and a brilliant mind.

It has been such a pleasure for me to watch him mature into a prince among preachers. I have no doubt that he is destined to become one of the most exceptional and influential church leaders in our time.

I salute you, Chad!

Congratulations on an excellent little book that has huge relevancy to our time!

*Rob Rufus—Founding Pastor,*
*City Church International, Hong Kong*

# PREFACE

The content of this little book came largely out of a short preaching series I undertook with Bayside Church in early 2009 through the book of Galatians. Arguably the most passionate of Paul's letters, in it the apostle describes himself as being both 'astonished' and 'perplexed' with the ease with which the Galatian believers were pressured into embracing and living by a perverted gospel—one which he describes as being 'no gospel at all' (Galatians 1:6–7; Galatians 4:20).

The epistle reaches an oft-quoted climax in the opening verse of the fifth chapter, when Paul appeals to his readers to 'stand firm' and avoid falling into slavery and away from grace (Galatians 5:1). The word he uses here literally means to remain *completely static and stationary,* unmoved in a steadfast stance of stillness and stability.

Yet, in what appears to be contrary to this passionate appeal to a sturdy stillness, Paul continues in the following verses to urge them to be anything but inactive!

Rather, he instructs these believers to devote themselves wholeheartedly to a lifestyle of submission to the Spirit's leadership; to actively serve and share with one another; to sacrificially sow good deeds at every possible opportunity; to recognise their redemptive role in restoring God's family, while at the same time, always taking responsibility to carry the specific 'load' God had called them to bear (Galatians 6:1–10).

The question then needs to be asked: Do we stand still, or do we get active and move on?

In my Galatians series I presented it this way:

- Concerning our *position* 'in Christ'—that legal standing we receive in the spirit realm the moment we are justified through faith in Jesus—we are to remain still and steadfast. Our confidence before God, and the great privilege we have to access His presence and provisions both in this life and the next, comes only because of who He declares us to be *in Jesus*. In this conviction we are to steadfastly stand, unmoved and unshaken in the true Gospel of Christ.

- But concerning our *posture* as we walk and work 'with Christ'—the attitudes we appropriate and actions we undertake in cooperation with and obedience to Him—we are to be anything but still. God has called us to 'front-footed Christianity'! Knowing that Christ has taken hold of us, we are to *press on* to take hold of everything He has called us to possess and obtain!

Our *position* in Christ—or more specifically, our *faith* in that heavenly position—is to remain unchanging and firm. But our *posture*—how we live out our life on this planet—is one of constant movement and flexibility.

Every spiritual blessing has been given and made available to us 'in Christ' (Ephesians 1:3). God's blessings are our privilege, and they are there *for the taking*. However, we still play a part in determining the degree to which we lay hold of these promises.

Consider, for a moment, the two brothers in Jesus' Parable of the Prodigal Son—which I prefer to describe as the Parable of the Kissing Father—in Luke 15. Despite their inaccurate conceptions about their dad, and the subsequent attitudes and actions these convictions cultivated, at no point did either brother lose their identity as sons of the father or as rightful heirs of his estate.

Their personal *experience* of his love and blessings was limited by their unhelpful thought patterns and life choices, but their *entitlement* to the father's presence and provision remained constant. Their position as sons never changed.

The primary purpose of this book is to convince you that the *privilege* of God's promised blessing is yours because of your position in Christ. Understanding your entitlement to God's promises is an essential starting point for your ongoing and ever-increasing experience of such blessing.

In fiscal terms, my intention is not to lay out for you a list of instructions on how to withdraw funds from your account, but rather, to see you firmly established in the knowledge that the account is in your name in the first place!

The Promised Land is yours; the Lord has given it to you—now go and 'take possession' of it (Numbers 33:53)!

Another key motivation for producing this book is my passion for hermeneutics, the science and practice of biblical interpretation. Understanding God's major *covenants*—also referred to as *testaments*—is critical in this process as we seek to rightly divide the Word of Truth.

A friendly warning however; you may come to discover that the Bible is best divided into three testaments, rather than two, as most of us have been trained to view it. You will find the Scripture references at the title page of each chapter particularly helpful in this regard.

Finally, please give special attention to the explanatory notes and references to assist in further study and clarification of the truths presented.

While this book is designed such that it can be read through in one sitting, it is my hope that it will serve also as a valuable reference to which you return again and again, as you seek to 'grow in the grace and knowledge of our Lord and Savior Jesus Christ. To him be glory both now and forever! Amen' (2 Peter 3:18).

Blessya,

*Chad M. Mansbridge*

# INTRODUCTION

## Abraham, Moses, and Jesus

### Three Covenants—Three Conditions

*For no matter how many promises God has made,*
***they are "Yes" in Christ****. And so through him the*
*"Amen" is spoken by us to the glory of God. Now it*
*is God who makes both us and you* ***stand firm in***
***Christ****. He anointed us, set his seal of ownership*
*on us, and put his Spirit in our hearts as a deposit,*
*guaranteeing what is to come.*

**2 Corinthians 1:20–22**

Of all the characters found throughout the pages of the Old Testament; of all the prophets and priests, rulers and kings; of all the great men and women of faith; the friends, followers, and even foes of God; of all those who shaped Old Testament history and those who recorded it; these two men, *Abraham* and *Moses*, are, second only to Christ Himself, the most mentioned and most frequently referred to characters in the pages of the New.

The reason for this is simple.

Abraham and Moses represent the two great *pre-Calvary covenants* offered by God to mankind. These two covenants, together with the covenant ratified by Jesus Himself, are discussed at great length in the New Testament Scriptures, and particularly in the letters of Paul, largely because the Christians of the first century had great difficulty discerning between them.

There seemed to be a great degree of confusion in the early Christian Church as to the difference between Jesus Christ's covenant of grace (the 'New Covenant'), the law-keeping covenant of Moses (the 'Old Covenant'), and the covenant promised to Abraham.

It would seem that this same confusion still exists throughout the Church today.

The purpose of this book is to present a very simple explanation of the main differences between these forms of relationship with God, and specifically to identify what it is (*or what it was*) that 'qualifies' people to access God's promised blessings.

Namely, the promise of His presence and provisions.

My proposal is as straightforward as this:

- Under the Abrahamic Covenant, God's promises become your right and inheritance because of your *pedigree*.

- Under the Mosaic Law Covenant, God's promises are your right and inheritance because of your *performance*.

- But under the New Covenant Agreement, through the Gospel of Jesus, God's promised blessings are your right and inheritance purely because of your *position*.

As we have just read, all His promises 'are "Yes" *in Christ*.'

In this book you will discover that through the complete redemptive work and saving power of Jesus as revealed in the Gospel, it is God Himself, and God alone, who qualifies us to share in His rich and eternal inheritance.

The question is, are you 'in Christ'?

If so, you qualify for all of God's precious and powerful promises, despite your family pedigree or fluctuating performance.

But it hasn't always been that way...

# CHAPTER 1

## The Abrahamic Covenant

### from Abraham to Joseph
### Genesis 12–50

*I will make you into a great nation and **I will bless you**; I will make your name great, and you will be a blessing. I will bless those who bless you, and whoever curses you I will curse; and all peoples on earth will be blessed through you … I will make you very fruitful; I will make nations of you, and kings will come from you. I will establish my covenant as an everlasting covenant between me and you **and your descendants after you** for the generations to come, to be your God and the God of your descendants after you.*

**Genesis 12:2–3; 17:6–7**

Of all the heroes recorded in the great Hall of Faith of Hebrews 11, Abraham is given by far the most time and attention. In the sixth chapter, the Hebrew authors also identify him as one whom we, as New Covenant believers, should 'imitate' because of his faith (Hebrews 6:12–15).

Even the prophet Isaiah encourages those who 'seek the Lord' and 'pursue righteousness' to look to Abraham as a mentor and model (Isaiah 51:1–2).

Undoubtedly, there is great value in us possessing an accurate understanding of Abraham's faith and personal walk with the

Lord, including the promises God offered him in his homeland, his encounter with the royal priest Melchizedek in the Valley of Shaveh, and the oath God later swore at Mount Moriah where Isaac was placed on the altar. However, since space here does not allow for a detailed exploration or explanation of these particular subjects, my intention is to highlight *one simple aspect* of the Abrahamic Covenant.

Namely, that between Genesis Chapter 12 (some would say Genesis 22) and Exodus 19, the promise of God's special blessings was guaranteed only to those who were of the family line of Abraham, and so long as you were an heir of Abraham, you 'qualified' as a rightful heir of God's presence and provisions, but never of His wrath, vengeance, or curse.

> **My intention is to highlight one simple aspect of the Abrahamic Covenant**

In other words, under the Abrahamic Agreement, the promise of God's blessing was not dependent upon your performance, but simply your pedigree. God's favour was not guaranteed to those who *behaved right*, but to those who were *born right*—to those who were born into, or identified themselves as belonging to, the family line of Abraham.

Understanding this then, gives us insight into God's purpose for the institution of male circumcision, which He gave to Abraham just prior to the birth of Isaac, his first son and heir.[1]

There are two things here I believe are well worth noting. Firstly, circumcision was not a *condition* for God's covenant blessings. After all, God had already been blessing Abraham for some twenty years prior to this instruction! Rather, it was a '*sign*' of the covenant that Abraham was already walking in (Genesis 17:11–12).[2]

The second important observation is this: God didn't need Abraham to be circumcised for *His* benefit. It would be ludicrous to think that God was fearful of forgetting who Abraham was, and so initiated circumcision as a means to distinguish him from all the other nomadic shepherds of the day! Clearly, Abraham's circumcision was not for God's sake.

Rather, circumcision was a sign for Abraham's benefit, and particularly for the benefit of his descendants and male heirs after him. It was an *imposed identity marker* for Abraham's sons and acted as a personal daily reminder to his heirs as to their family line, their history with El Shaddai, and the promises that belonged to them as a result of that pedigree.

> **Circumcision served as an ongoing reminder of God's covenant promises**

Like Cain's mark, Noah's rainbow, and Moses' Passover meal, the sign of circumcision served as an *ongoing reminder* to God's people of His covenant promises to them.[3]

You see, God doesn't need to be reminded of His promises—as if He would ever forget them! But His people often do. Which is why (I believe) God instituted this practice.

Every day, no matter where life's journey took them, Abraham's male heirs would see this permanent and very personal mark on their bodies and again be *reminded of who they were* and how they were distinguished from the nations around them, all because of their pedigree. And, as those covenant promises were recalled to their remembrance, the 'faith and patience' required to take possession of them were renewed (Hebrews 6:12).[4]

So, the Lord continued to bless Abraham and his descendants, proving faithful to His covenant promises.

Now, please allow me to highlight another very significant and noteworthy observation.

After swearing His covenant oath to Abraham at Mount Moriah, God *never once* curses, rebukes, punishes, or judges Abraham or his descendants, despite their behaviour and, at times, very questionable morality.

While the Genesis account provides us with numerous examples along the way showing that God was *capable* of demonstrating His wrath against humanity, there is no scriptural record (prior to Exodus 19) that His anger was ever directed at Abraham or his heirs.

Think about it:

- Abraham flees from where God has called him, blatantly lies on two separate occasions about the true identity of his wife, allowing other men to have non-consensual sex with her, and all because he is cowardly, fearful, and self-centred. Yet not once does God curse, or even (it seems) rebuke him for this behaviour! Instead, God continues to be faithful to His covenant promises, *blessing Abraham* and cursing his enemies.[5]

- Abraham's son and heir Isaac is likewise driven by fear to lie about his wife under very similar circumstances. Yet again, God never corrects his behaviour or punishes Isaac, but rather continues to bless and prosper him to such a lavish extreme that his great wealth causes his Philistine neighbours to become irrepressibly envious.[6]

- Then there's Jacob, whose very name means 'deceiver'. He deceives his way into Isaac's blessing, which God honours even though he lied to get it. Then, together with his wife Rachel, he tricks his father-in-law out of his possessions and pilfers his religious artefacts, all the while blatantly denying any impropriety. But yet again, God never once rebukes or judges them for this behaviour. In fact, God rebukes Laban for planning to hurt Jacob, but never rebukes Jacob or Rachel for stealing from Laban.[7]

Again, evidence that God is relating to Jacob on the basis of his Abrahamic pedigree and not his behaviour.

- And then, there's Jacob's sons. Simeon and Levi deceive an entire city, making it vulnerable to their attack, and then proceed to murder its men and plunder its possessions and people. Reuben has illegitimate sex with one of his stepmothers, and while away on a business trip, Judah hires a shrine prostitute for his personal pleasure only to discover later that he had impregnated his own daughter-in-law, deliberately disguised to deceive him! Then finally, there is the envy-motivated murder plot of the brothers against Joseph, the selling of him into slavery, and the deliberate and elaborate lying to their ageing father about his fate.[8]

Yet amazingly, despite all this, God never rebukes, corrects, or judges any of them for this behaviour! Instead, He continues to be faithful to His covenant to Abraham, by blessing those who identified as his sons and heirs, *purely because of their pedigree.*[9]

# CHAPTER 2

## Israel 'under' Abraham

### from Egypt to Sinai
### Exodus 1–18

*The LORD did not set his affection on you and choose you because you were more numerous than other peoples, for you were the fewest of all peoples. But it was because **the LORD loved you and kept the oath he swore to your forefathers** that he brought you out with a mighty hand and redeemed you from the land of slavery, from the power of Pharaoh king of Egypt.*

### Deuteronomy 7:7–8

After the final chapter of Genesis draws to a close, the death of Jacob's sons and the passing of that entire generation, Israel's growing tribes cry out because of their slavery to the Egyptians. God hears their cries, is concerned about them, and because of His promise to their father Abraham, Yahweh rescues His people, who leave their oppressors healthy, wealthy, and whole![1]

And it is here, in the journey of the Israelite nation from Egypt towards Canaan, that the great contrast between the Abrahamic Covenant, and the soon-to-be-established Mosaic Law Covenant is so clearly seen.

One is a covenant whereby the promise of God's blessing is guaranteed simply because of their pedigree. The other is a covenant based on *pedigree plus performance.*

More on that later.

In Exodus 12, the plague on the firstborn passes through Egypt as a great and final sign of Yahweh's judgment on the Egyptian gods and on the enemies of His people. That night, however, the judgment *passes over* those who identified themselves as being of Abrahamic descent.

Similar to circumcision, the *identity mark* instituted in this instance involved blood. This blood was a sign *for the Israelites* that they were distinguished from the Egyptians purely because of their pedigree, and that God was rescuing them simply because of His gracious faithfulness to their forefathers.

Again, like circumcision, this sign was not for God's benefit!

God Himself had no need to be reminded of who His people were, as if He would ever forget, or never knew in the first place! This sign of shed blood was for *their benefit*, in that it would serve as an ongoing annual reminder for their descendants of the great act of deliverance God performed for them that night.[2]

> **The death of the Passover Lamb had nothing to do with forgiveness**

Now, please allow me to make this point very clear: the Passover meal and the shedding of the lamb's blood had absolutely *nothing to do with forgiveness.* The death of the Passover lamb had nothing to do with the sin or rebellion of God's people, or of atoning for any immorality or impurity in them. There is not one mention of sin, transgression, propitiation, substitution, or any other related terms in that entire story![3]

And the reason for that is simple: Like Abraham, Isaac, and Jacob, these Israelites were in a covenant of grace, where God was not counting their sins against them. The Law had not yet come to them, and 'where there is no law there is no transgression' (Romans 4:15). So far as God is concerned, 'sin is not taken into account when there is no law' (Romans 5:13).

So, when the Israelites left Egypt, God treated them as He did their forefathers. Despite their ungodly behaviour and consistently ungrateful attitude, God was faithful in *blessing them* with His presence and provisions, and *never once* cursed, punished, or judged them. That is, however, until they came to Sinai.

Here's a brief overview:

- In Exodus 14, the Israelites arrive at the banks of the Red Sea, and their first instinct is to complain to Moses about their situation. God, faithful as always, kindly and powerfully parts it for them.[4]

- In Exodus 15, they come to a place with bitter water, and again they whine and complain. So what does God do? Simple. He makes the water sweet for them.[5]

- In the next chapter they complain against Moses about not having enough food, and when God hears their grumbling, do you know what He does? Do you know what He does to show them 'who's in charge'? God very generously provides fresh food for them.

And this time, as He again meets their needs, God also provides a little 'test' for them. He gives instructions to them through Moses as to how exactly they should collect and store the manna, while at the same time instituting the observance of a 'day of

**God blesses them simply because they are children of Abraham**

rest, a holy Sabbath to the LORD'. The people, however, blatantly disobey God's commands and instructions, paying 'no attention' to what He had asked of them (Exodus 16:4, 20–23). [6] In response to this defiant arrogance and disrespect, *Moses gets angry* with the people. But do you know what God does? He continues to provide for them, despite their disobedience! He doesn't scold them, curse them, or punish them, nor does He withdraw His presence or provision from them.

God continues to bless His people *simply because* they are children of Abraham.

- In Exodus 17, they arrive in Rephidim and discover that there is no water to drink. Yet despite the fact the Lord had previously proved faithful with providing for them, do they approach God politely and trust Him for supernatural provision once more? Not at all. The community quarrels and grumbles and complains against Moses *again*, even threatening to stone their leader to death! So, what does God do? Yep, you guessed it! He provides for them from the rock and meets their need yet again. [7]

The reason for God's incredibly gracious treatment of them is clear and consistent with the Genesis account. As beneficiaries of the Abrahamic Covenant, God was not relating to these people on the basis of their behaviour but of their *birthright*.

Up to this point, His blessing was not conditional upon their performance, but simply their *pedigree*.

But all that was about to radically change.

# CHAPTER 3

## The Law-Keeping Covenant
### from Sinai to Simeon#
### Exodus 19–Matthew 1

*Now if you obey me fully and keep my covenant,* ***then*** *out of all nations you will be my treasured possession ...* ***If you pay attention to these laws*** *and are careful to follow them,* ***then*** *the LORD your God will keep his covenant of love with you, as he swore to your forefathers ... See, I am setting before you today a blessing and a curse—***the blessing if you obey the commands*** *of the LORD your God that I am giving you today;* ***the curse if you disobey...***

**Exodus 19:5; Deuteronomy 7:12; 11:26–28**

At Mount Sinai (or Horeb as it is also known) a *new* covenant was introduced through Moses. This was a *law-keeping covenant*, and it radically transformed the way God and His people related.

The promise of God's special blessing now required strict behavioural obedience to a long and exhaustive set of commands. A high *standard of performance* was introduced as a means to *earn the right* to what had previously been theirs simply because of their pedigree.

But that's not all.

*Failure* to meet the high-performance standards of this new agreement resulted in the withdrawal of the presence and provision of God, and also of the outpouring of His *burning anger.* When God's people fell short of the strict behavioural conditions of this covenant, it resulted in them experiencing firsthand—and for the first time in their national history—His wrath, fury, judgment, and curse.

What was once reserved for Abraham's enemies and foreigners to God's promises was now poured out upon Abraham's sons who failed to adhere to the conditions of this law-keeping agreement.

The way God related to His people changed in an instant. There was no 'grace period' given for them to get accustomed to this new arrangement. The change was radical, swift, and dramatic, and took them completely by surprise.

After the people agree to this new behaviour-dependent covenant with Yahweh in Exodus 19 and then confirm their commitment with a blood oath in Chapter 24, Moses returns up the mountain and over a period of forty days receives further instructions from God and, most significantly, the two stone tablets of the covenant, 'inscribed by the finger of God' (Exodus 31:18).[1]

Then, the very moment God placed these tablets in his hands, while still up on the mountaintop, God told Moses that He was about to completely destroy His people. Why? Because, although unknown to Moses at the time, the Israelites were worshipping a golden calf at the foot of the mountain and were disobeying the covenant commands God had just given them.[2]

With no 'first-chance warning' provided, God's anger burned against His people because of their idolatrous behaviour. Although they had *previously worshipped false gods* during their time in Egypt, and had acted in rebellious and defiant ways many times prior to this, for the very first time in recorded history God's anger was aroused against His covenant people.[3]

As a result, He 'struck the people with a plague', promised to 'blot' those who had sinned against Him out of His book, and 3,000 of Abraham's descendants were instantly put to death (Exodus 32:27–35).[4]

After receiving new stone tablets, Moses leads the people in a six-month building project. Once complete, the glory cloud of God descends over the newly constructed tabernacle for a period of seven consecutive weeks, and a priest-led sacrificial system is established, designed to alleviate God's judgment against His people's ongoing rebellion.[5]

Then finally, after almost a year camped at Mt. Sinai, God's glory cloud moves on, the trumpets are blown, and the journey towards the Land of Promise continues.

What happens next is striking:

- In Numbers 11, within the first three days of their travels, the people complain about their hardships 'in the hearing of the LORD' (Numbers 11:1). Now this should come as no surprise to us. After all, they were *constantly* complaining during their travels from Egypt to Sinai, remember? Their behaviour is no different now. What is dramatically different, however, is *how God responds to them*. Prior to Exodus 19, when they complained and grumbled, God continued to bless them. But now, post-Sinai, do you know what God does as a result of their ungrateful attitude and behaviour? He sends fire from Heaven and kills a bunch of them.

- Later on in that same chapter, they wail about the quality and variety of food God has provided for them. The Scripture says, 'The LORD became exceedingly angry' against the people (Numbers 11:10), and He struck them with a plague, resulting in the death of many.

- In Numbers 12, Miriam murmurs against Moses, again arousing the Lord's burning anger. As a result, God 'spit[s] in her face' (Numbers 12:14) and she is cursed with leprosy.

- In the following two chapters, Moses sends twelve spies into Canaan. Only Caleb and Joshua bring back a positive report. The remaining spies 'spread among the Israelites a bad report about the land' and, as a result, were 'struck down and died of a plague before the LORD' (Numbers 13:32; 14:37).

- In Numbers 15, a man is found 'gathering wood on the Sabbath' (Numbers 15:32). The people inquire of the Lord what should be done about this, and God responds by commanding he be stoned to death.

- In Numbers 16, a man named Korah, together with a group of 250 community leaders, oppose and challenge Moses' leadership. As a result of their defiance, God opens the ground, swallows up Korah and his entire household alive, and then sends out fire from His presence that burns Korah's followers to death! The following day the rest of the Israelite community grumble against Moses, blaming him for this dramatic series of events, and God responds by sending a plague which kills a further 14,700 Israelites that day.[6]

- A short time later the community again grumble against God and Moses because of their food and water, and God responds this time in a similar fashion to His previous judgments on Egypt. He sends among His own people a plague of 'venomous snakes' (Numbers 21:6). Yet again, many of Abraham's descendants die as a result of this judgment and curse.

Now, please answer me this…

What is God's problem? Why the sudden change in His behaviour and demeanour toward His people? Why the abrupt outbursts of rage and demonstrations of wrath? Has God experienced a hormonally motivated *mood swing*? Does Yahweh suffer from a *multiple personality disorder*? Has God *changed*?

Between Egypt and Sinai God does nothing but *bless His people*. He demonstrates nothing but love and compassion and generosity to them, despite their rebellious behaviour and wicked attitudes!

Yet now, in the Book of Numbers, just a few months later, God is treating them completely different!

It seems that whenever they put one foot out of line, God curses them, punishes them, and judges them! For many, He does not even give the time or opportunity to repent! His vengeance comes fast and fierce.

One thing we know for sure is that the people haven't changed.

**God's curse now becomes the inheritance of His own kids!**

They are still of Abrahamic descent, and they are acting no different to how they did on the other side of the mountain! Pre-Sinai, they worship false gods, break the Sabbath, murmur and complain, grumble against God and the leadership of Moses, and yet God never even comes close to punishing them. In fact, He doesn't even rebuke them. Just like He did with Abraham, Isaac, and Jacob, God never even recalls or highlights the fact that they are behaving in a way which grossly misrepresents and grieves Him.

Yet after Sinai, just a few months later, the *same behaviour* results in God's anger burning against them—expressed in cursing, punishment, wrath, vengeance, pain, and death!

*What is going on?*

Well, the fact is this: God hasn't (in Himself) changed, and His people haven't (yet) changed. The only thing that has changed at this point is the *form of relationship* they are in.

The first was a *covenant of grace*, where God's *undeserved blessing* became their right and inheritance simply because of their Abrahamic pedigree, and where His vengeance and wrath were reserved for those *outside* of this lineage, and particularly for those who would curse Abraham's tribe.

The second is a *law-keeping covenant*, where God's blessing and favour is promised to those who are not only *born right*, but also *behave right*. But more than that, it is a covenant where *God's curse* becomes the inheritance not only of Abraham's enemies, but also of those in Abraham's own family who fail to perform the exacting requirements of this new agreement.

Over the next fourteen centuries, as the story of God's people unfolds, the ramifications of their inability to keep the conditions of this Mosaic covenant are repeatedly suffered.

When, from time to time, they performed obedience to the Law to an acceptable standard, the children of Israel experienced a measure of the blessing of their God.

But when they failed, as they often did, the Lord would desert them, hand them over to disaster, devastation, defeat, doom, death, and destruction, and even divorce Himself from them because of their unfaithfulness to His covenant.[7]

Until finally, after many years of labouring under the curse and tyranny of the Law and its constant demands, angelic hosts appear from Heaven and herald the birth of Israel's promised Messiah.[8]

# CHAPTER 4

## Out with the Old... in with the New

### from John to Jesus
### Matthew 1–Acts 1

*The Law and the Prophets **were until John**; since then **the good news** of the kingdom of God is preached, and everyone forces his way into it.*

**Luke 16:16 (ESV)**

As the immediate prophetic forerunner to Jesus' earthly ministry, the one who came 'in the spirit and power of Elijah' to 'prepare the way for the Lord' (Luke 1:17; Mark 1:3), John the Baptiser provides us with a profound revelation of the identity of the Son of God, and of the implications of His coming for mankind.[1]

Firstly, John announces Him as 'the Lamb of God, who *takes away* the sin of the world' (John 1:29).[2]

Like the lamb of Passover, Jesus' spilt blood would be remembered by God's covenant people in the sharing of a meal for generations to come.[3] And, like the lambs of the priesthood, Jesus in His death would pay the ultimate price as a payment for the transgressions of God's people against His holy law.[4]

But far more than that...

Jesus' sacrifice would put an end to the entire Old Covenant sacrificial system, in that it would literally 'take away' the sin of its beneficiaries (Hebrews 9:28), eliminating the need for any future atoning sacrifices to be offered. Whereas the Levitical lambs would merely alleviate God's wrath for a time, this lamb would 'for all time' *remove sin* from the heavenly accounts of those who would believe (Hebrews 10:12).[5]

As John the apostle would later declare, 'he appeared so that he might *take away our sins*' (1 John 3:5).

Secondly, the prophet John declares Jesus as the one who would 'baptize with the Holy Spirit' (John 1:33).[6]

You see, the content of his gospel was plain: 'Repent, for *the kingdom of heaven is at hand*' (Matthew 3:2 ESV).[7] But the substance of John's gospel was a person. The one who would pay for our sin so that we might *enter* Heaven, is the same one who pours out His Spirit so that we might *experience* (and even *effect and enforce*) Heaven on earth.

With both moral acts of purity and (after His baptism) miraculous acts of power, for thirty-three years the Son of Man would serve as the perfect representation of God 'in the flesh', thus completing one major aspect of His earthly assignment—to reveal the name and nature of His Father.[8]

Then, while nailed to a cross, suspended between Heaven and earth upon a hill called Golgotha, after fulfilling what had been prophesied concerning Him, Jesus would utter these much-anticipated words before His death: '*It is finished*' (John 19:30).

Now, let me ask you… *what* had finished?

Certainly, Jesus' work hadn't finished. Not by a long shot!

He hadn't been buried yet, been raised from the dead or broken out of the tomb in His resurrection glory; He hadn't 'preached to the spirits in prison' (1 Peter 3:19) or entered

> **Jesus, the Lamb of God who takes away sin… "It is finished!"**

Heaven as High Priest on our behalf leading 'captives in his train' (Ephesians 4:8); He hadn't yet sat down at the right hand of the Majesty, or poured out God's Spirit as promised; He hadn't appeared to Paul, Peter, or the other apostles; and He most certainly hadn't come again in His heavenly glory and splendour.[9]

Jesus had a great deal more to do!

So, what was He referring to as He declared, *'It is finished'*?

The moment He uttered these climactic words, the curtain in the temple was torn in two—from Heaven to earth—signifying *the end of the Old Covenant era* and the dawning of a new age where access to God's presence and provision is made freely available.[10]

The Old Covenant system introduced through Moses, mediated by angels, and maintained through multiple generations, *was now redundant* and soon to be replaced![11]

---

By the shed blood and broken body of God's Suffering Servant, a new and superior covenant is introduced at Calvary, and inaugurated fifty days later at Pentecost.[12]

A *new covenant,* which 'sets aside' the now 'obsolete' covenant of Moses (Hebrews 8:13; 10:9).

A *right-standing relationship* with God where pedigree and performance count for nothing.[13]

An agreement with God that is not based on being born right or behaving right.

An arrangement whereby all of God's covenant promises are 'Yes' to those who simply *believe right.*

A covenant *the Father cut with the man Christ Jesus,* on behalf of the entire human race, whose benefits become the right and inheritance of those who are *positioned in Him.*

# CHAPTER 5

## The New Covenant
### from Pentecost to Eternity
### Acts 2–Revelation 22

*Remember that you were at that time separated from Christ, alienated from the commonwealth of Israel and strangers to the covenants of promise, having no hope and without God in the world. But now **in Christ Jesus** you who once were far off have been brought near by the blood of Christ ... **In him we have obtained an inheritance...***

### Ephesians 2:12–13; 1:11 (ESV)

Friends, family, and fellow followers of Jesus, I have good news for you! We are God's people, His treasured possession and rightful heirs of His glorious presence, His generous provisions, and all other covenant blessings, simply because we are *in Christ*.

In other words, our relationship with God is based on our *position*—our position in the person of Jesus.

Despite your family pedigree, despite your fluctuating performance, regardless of your paternal background or pious behaviour, God has agreed to bless you and relate to you purely on the basis of your secure position, 'in the Beloved' (Ephesians 1:6 ESV).

You see, as the only begotten Son of God, *Jesus has the perfect pedigree.*[1]

He has the perfect credentials in regard to His family line and history. And, when you are placed and positioned *in Christ*, His perfect pedigree becomes yours. You become brothers of Jesus, as His Father becomes your Father.[2]

You become a co-heir with Christ, and He gives you the full rights of spiritual sonship.[3]

Not only that, but Jesus is 'The Offspring' to which the Abrahamic promises were made. Paul teaches that ultimately the promises to Abraham were made to one (singular) Offspring, not to many (plural) offsprings.[4] This is particularly true for the promise of possessing the earth and blessing the nations of the world through the gift of righteousness.[5]

> **Through the Gospel, you are 'in Christ'... and He has the perfect pedigree**

Therefore, since Jesus is the rightful heir of Abraham's blessings, those who are placed *in Him* are now automatically considered co-heirs with Christ of the same promises!

In other words, although Abraham had the kind of faith that was willing to lay Isaac on the altar, you don't have to possess that same faith to be guaranteed the Abrahamic promises.

You don't have to have the kind of faith that makes you willing to kill your son; you just have to have faith that God was willing to kill His Son.

The moment you have faith in Jesus, you are placed *into Him*. You are permanently placed and positioned in the one who is 'the Seed' and rightful heir of Abraham. You are baptised into, clothed and covered with, the one who has the perfect pedigree.[6]

And so, the promises God made to Abraham and his offspring now belong to those who are placed into Christ. Because Jesus *perfectly qualifies* for Abraham's blessings, so do those who are found *in Him*!

The promise of greatness, fruitfulness, influence, and significance; the promise of great reward, and a blessing that is contagious and world-reaching; the promise of protection, vindication, and abundant provision; the promise of a great personal legacy, land possession, and the privilege of walking blameless in His presence, all belong to those who believe in Jesus.[7]

But wait, there's more.

As the spotless and faultless Lamb of God, *Jesus also has the perfect performance*. Although tempted in every way as we are, He was without sin.[8] The Scripture says, 'He committed no sin, and no deceit was found in his mouth' (1 Peter 2:22).[9]

Unlike the descendants of Abraham, not only was Jesus *born right*, He also perfectly *behaved right*.

In His life, the man Christ Jesus perfectly performed obedience to the Law. In His death, He also perfectly performed as a payment for every disobedience to the Law.

So, Jesus, by His perfect performance, has been counted worthy of inheriting all of God's blessings as promised in the Mosaic Law Covenant, and never again inheriting or experiencing the curse, wrath, anger, and judgment the Law demanded for disobedience. His once-for-all complete payment for sin at Calvary means that He will *never* taste of that punishment ever again.

The same is true for those who are found *in Him*, who have been declared forever holy by His sacrifice.[10] We too, because of our *position in Christ*, are rightful heirs of the blessings of God as described in the Mosaic Law, and never of the curses or judgments![11]

What God promised Israel as reward for their obedience is now the right and inheritance of the New Covenant believer *because of Christ's obedience* on our behalf.

> **Jesus Christ perfectly performed and satisfied the entire Law on our behalf**

The promise of a long and prosperous life; the promise of His special blessing and favour upon our families, economics, investments, possessions, and health; the promise of 'abundant prosperity' upon all the work of our hands, making us 'the head, not the tail', 'at the top, never at the bottom' (Deuteronomy 28:11–13); and the promise of God delighting in us—His people, His portion, and His most treasured possession.[12]

Because of Jesus' perfect performance, these wonderful Old Covenant promises are 'Yes' to those in Christ. If you are in Christ, *you qualify* for these blessings!

But yet again, there's more.

Not only are the pedigree-based promises of Abraham and the performance-based promises of Moses our inheritance, in the New Covenant a whole new set of promises become ours as well!

Through the Gospel of Jesus, God promises to forgive our wickedness and never recall or remember our sins again. In fact, not only are all debts forgiven and wiped completely clean, but God Himself credits our account with the perfect righteousness of Christ, so that we share *the same right standing* before the Father as does Jesus Himself![13]

As a result of His 'everlasting kindness', expressed in the substitutionary suffering and sacrifice of His Son, God promises to never be angry with His people again, to never remove His unfailing love or this 'covenant of peace' from those who stand justified

> **In Christ, we share the same 'right-standing' before God as Jesus Himself!**

before Him because of their knowledge of Christ (Isaiah 54:8–10). Unlike the now obsolete Law Covenant, this is an '*everlasting covenant*' where God promises to 'never stop' doing good to His people (Jeremiah 32:40).

In the New Covenant, God's empowering and intoxicating presence becomes our privileged portion, both now and for all eternity, and serves as the distinguishing mark of those who belong to Him.[14]

---

And it's not because we were *born right*.

It's not because we *behave right*.

It's simply because we *believe right*.

As Jesus Himself once said, we fulfil the work that God *requires* of us when we 'believe in the one he has sent' (John 6:29).

As a result of placing our trust in the one 'who had no sin [but became] sin for us, so that *in him* we might become the righteousness of God', we can now 'approach God with freedom and confidence' (2 Corinthians 5:21; Ephesians 3:12).

The privilege of free and uninhibited access to the supernatural presence and provision of God is ours, purely because we are placed and permanently positioned 'in Christ'.

In this everlasting and vastly superior covenant, *God Himself* has unmistakably and irreversibly '*qualified you*' to share in the eternal riches of His promised blessings (Colossians 1:12).

# CONCLUSION

## God Qualifies You!
### from Today On

*May you be strengthened with all power, according to his glorious might, for all endurance and patience with joy, **giving thanks to the Father, who has qualified you** to share in the inheritance of the saints in light. He has delivered us from the domain of darkness and transferred us to the kingdom of his beloved Son, in whom we have redemption, the forgiveness of sins.*

**Colossians 1:11–14 (ESV)**

In the words of Paul, the great first-century apostle, 'What, then, shall we say in response to this?' (Romans 8:31).

Well, for a start, praise God for such a great salvation! What an awesome Gospel! What an incredible covenant the Father has offered to us through Jesus!

That the precious promise of God's personal presence and plentiful provisions are our privilege and portion purely because of our position in Christ is truly amazing!

Regardless of our performance or pedigree, our background or behaviour, the blessings of God become our birthright based entirely upon the fact that we have been born again by the Spirit, baptised into Christ, clothed with His holiness, and granted the gracious gift of His righteousness through faith in His Gospel.

To describe this new covenant as 'better' than and 'superior to' (Hebrews 7:22; 8:6) the law-keeping covenant of Moses is, in my estimation, one of the greatest understatements of the Scriptures!

To consider the Old and New Covenants synonymous is nothing short of ludicrous![1]

To receive the New, then turn back and embrace the Old, is foolishness.[2]

To confuse the two, by not 'rightly dividing' them (2 Timothy 2:15 NKJV), is ignorance.[3]

But to deliberately mix and co-associate these covenants as being both relevant to the life and practice of the Church, is the very essence of Christian heresy and doctrinal divergence.[4]

---

I trust that you would discover from today a greater freedom and confidence to embrace and take possession of the many great and glorious promises of God, which are 'Yes' to you because you are positioned *in Christ* (2 Corinthians 1:20).

All that's left for you to do now is say, 'Amen—so be it', and to '*press on*' through whatever challenges may come your way, to take hold of all those things for which Christ Jesus took a firm hold of you (Philippians 3:12).

*Finally, my brothers, rejoice in the Lord! It is no trouble for me to write the same things to you again, and it is a safeguard for you. Watch out for those dogs, those men who do evil, those mutilators of the flesh. For it is we who are the circumcision, we who worship by the Spirit of God, who glory in Christ Jesus, and who put no confidence in the flesh—though I myself have reasons for such confidence. If anyone else thinks he has reasons to put confidence in the flesh, I have more: circumcised on the eighth day, of the people of Israel, of the tribe of Benjamin, a Hebrew of Hebrews **[the 'perfect pedigree']**; in regard to the law, a Pharisee; as for zeal, persecuting the church; as for legalistic righteousness, faultless **[the 'perfect performance']**. But whatever was to my profit I now consider loss for the sake of Christ. What is more, I consider everything a loss compared to the surpassing greatness of knowing Christ Jesus my Lord, for whose sake I have lost all things. I consider them rubbish, that I may gain Christ and be found in him **[the 'perfect position']**, not having a righteousness of my own that comes from the law, but that which is through faith in Christ—the righteousness that comes from God and is by faith. I want to know Christ...*

**Philippians 3:1–10**

# FINAL THOUGHTS

## The Progression of God's Covenants
### from Infancy to Adulthood

*So then, **the law was our guardian until Christ came**, in order that we might be justified by faith. But now that faith has come, we are no longer under a guardian, for **in Christ Jesus you are all sons of God**, through faith ... we also, **when we were children**, were enslaved to the elementary principles of the world. But when the fullness of time had come, God sent forth his Son, born of woman, born under the law, to redeem those **who were under the law**, so that we might receive adoption **as sons.***

**Galatians 3:24–26; 4:3–5 (ESV)**

I'd like to leave you with these final thoughts for your consideration.

Abraham was well along in years at the time he entered into covenant with God and became the father of our faith. However, Abraham's descendants, as an *identifiable nation* under God's headship, were still very much in their infancy prior to Sinai.

And in some ways, God seemed to treat them *like a baby*.

True, He never punished or cursed them for their poor behaviour, but to not even rebuke or correct them on how they conducted themselves? Isn't that a little irresponsible of God? To allow them to 'get away' with behaviour that so poorly represented the integrity of His character?

For all we know, God never once attempted to adjust their ethics or moral values and practice. Did God simply *not care* how they behaved?

Early stories in Genesis reveal a God who *is concerned* about the behaviour of those created in His likeness. For example, the account of Noah in Genesis 6 describes how it grieved and pained God to see how human wickedness had caused such violence on the earth.[1]

> **Prior to Sinai, Abraham's nation were in their infancy**

Later, we read of the sin of Sodom being 'so grievous' (Genesis 18:20) that, despite Abraham's plea, God destroyed the entire city![2] This leaves no doubt that prior to the arrival of the Law Covenant, God has *always cared* about the manner in which human beings have conducted themselves.

Moreover, a simple reading of the New Testament will quite quickly show us that God *certainly* concerns Himself with the conduct of His Church, with the behaviour of those who bear His holy name.[3]

I'd like to propose to you that prior to Sinai, God treated and dealt with His people as an *infant nation*.

No good parent ever punishes or curses their newborn baby for its selfish or ungrateful attitudes. Nor do we rebuke, correct, or attempt to adjust an infant's *moral* behaviour.

Despite a baby's self-centred conduct, and constant grumbling and complaining, a good parent will overlook such behaviour (which for an adult would be completely out of place, but for a baby is acceptable) and continue to meet the infant's needs.

We wait until the infant grows to become a child, before corrections or consequences play a part in our parenting.[4]

As we have just read, in Galatians Chapters 3 and 4, Paul describes the Jewish nation (those who were 'under the supervision of the law') as *children*, whereas he identifies the Christian nation (those who are 'in Christ Jesus') as *sons* (Galatians 3:23–4:7).[5]

The distinction he makes here between these two identities—that of a 'child' (Greek: *nēpios*), and that of a 'son' (Greek: *huios*)—is very deliberate, and reveals a profound truth.

He explains how the Law acted (among other things) much like a nanny or a schoolmaster for the Jewish people, always telling them what to do and keeping their behaviour in line. However, the Law *kept them as children* and never allowed them to grow up into the *full rights and privileges* of spiritual adulthood.[6]

So, in many respects, says Paul, they were not much different to *slaves* in the house. Sure, they were of the right *pedigree* and so had some sense of promised ownership to the Father's estate, but as children, so long as they remained under the constant *guardianship of the Law*, they never had the right or ability to freely access the full provisions of God's house.

Experiencing the manifest and intimate presence of God; the voice of prophecy, dreams, and visions; the ability to personally demonstrate miracles, and to experience the ongoing guidance of the indwelling Spirit in their hearts; these privileges, and many others, were not readily accessible to God's *children* under the Law. In fact, they were reserved only for a chosen few.

The New Covenant, however, *redefines our identity* in a radical way.

Paul's point is that because of our position in Christ (despite our race, occupation, or gender) the New Covenant believer is a fully-fledged *adult son* in God's house. We are *not children* in God's house (at least that is not his point in Galatians 3–4), the context here is that we are *adult heirs*.

As such, we have the full rights as heirs of God's presence and provisions, to draw on the promise of the Spirit; to operate in the power and authority of our Father; and to bless the nations of the world.[7]

My proposal is this:

- Under Abraham, God's people were *like babies*. They had little or no interest and desire to represent Him well. Their motives were predominantly selfish, like an infant's, and God *never corrected this*.

- Under the Law, God's people were *like children*. They had a tutor—a pedagogue—to keep them in line. They behaved as they did because their guardian demanded obedience, and they were punished when they failed.

- But now, in Christ, God's people are *adult sons*. We are those who possess the family inheritance rights as fully fledged adults. At the same time, we also have a responsibility to represent our Father and family well and are *called and expected* to extend His influence and kingdom on the earth.

With this analogy we see that God doesn't treat or view the Christian nation as babies, nor like immature children. *God sees us and treats us like adult sons*. He calls us 'fellow workers' together with Him (2 Corinthians 6:1) and sends us out into the world entrusting us with the responsibilities of *stewarding*

> **Those 'in Christ' possess the full rights of *adult* sons and heirs**

*His authority and property* in a way that honours His name and extends the boundaries of His kingly estate.[8]

Consequently, as mature adults, we have an *inbuilt desire* to submit to His instructions and live according to His intentions, because we understand that doing so brings pleasure to His heart and glory to His name.[9]

Believing that we have been commissioned by Christ as representatives of our Father, and ambassadors of His heavenly government, we 'make every effort' to *live holy*, so that, as a result of our character and conduct, others will 'see the Lord' and find His Gospel 'attractive' (Hebrews 12:14; Titus 2:10).[10]

As adults, we no longer require the Law as an *external source*, tutoring and supervising us along the way. In fact, God's desires and priorities are now written on the *tablets of our hearts*.[11] We simply get on with the family business, embracing both the rights and responsibilities of our adulthood.

And we are increasingly aware of what our Father's plans, passions, and preferences are because we are in intimate relationship with Him, thanks to the Spirit within us who calls out 'Abba, Father' (Galatians 4:6), and because of Jesus, our living example, who calls us 'friends' and 'brothers' (John 15:15; Hebrews 2:11).[12]

---

Through the Gospel, God's covenant privileges are no longer ours because of our pedigree or performance, but simply because of our position *in Christ*.

And with those rights come certain responsibilities because God is no longer treating His covenant nation as infants or children but as fully fledged adult sons, who are called to 'be about [our] Father's business' (Luke 2:49 NKJV)—being found in His presence and being faithful in stewarding His provisions.

*Selah.*

# A PERSONAL NOTE

Hey there, thanks for reading my book.

Before you go, I was hoping you could help me with something.

Since its first print run in 2010, *He Qualifies You!* has been a blessing to Christians of all streams and stripes. Today, it is being read in multiple languages and distributed in a growing number of developing-world contexts, helping pastors and people alike discover the liberating truth of the new covenant Gospel while learning to view the Scriptures from a whole-Bible perspective.

One of the best ways you can help spread the word is by *leaving an online review* on your favourite bookseller's website or platform. I would really appreciate you doing this.

Here are a few examples from readers who have offered five-star reviews on Amazon:

- A tiny book that packs an incredible punch!—C. M. Marais, 2012
- This is a great little book—Doug, 2015
- Highly recommend this book—Truth Seeker, 2018
- WOW, a short but LIFE-CHANGING BOOK—Robin, 2019
- Love this book. Simple to the point. Easy to understand— Norma, 2020
- Outstanding! Short and concise, simple yet extremely potent—Fanen, 2020

It may seem like a small thing, but it helps BIG. Much like this book, I suppose.

Also, I'd like to *offer you a little gift* in appreciation of your readership. Details can be found at www.chadmansbridge.com/hequalifiesyoubonus

Blessya heaps,

Chad M. Mansbridge

# NOTES

### Chapter 1: The Abrahamic Covenant

1.    Genesis 17:18–21; 21:12–13; 22:2, 12, 16. While Ishmael was, in fact, Abram's first biological child, God Himself never refers to him as Abram's *son*. He opts rather to describe Ishmael simply as 'the boy', 'your offspring', and 'the son of the maidservant'. Once Ishmael is banished from Abram's household, God calls *Isaac* 'your son, your *only* son'.

2.    See also Romans 4:11. Later, under the Old Covenant given at Sinai, circumcision became one of many commands *conditional* to qualify for God's blessing (Leviticus 12:3). With circumcision featuring prominently in both the Abrahamic and Mosaic covenants, it is no wonder first-century Christians—particularly those with Jewish backgrounds—struggled with Paul's teaching that it was now an utterly insignificant observation for the Church (Galatians 5:6; 6:15).

3.    Cain's mark (Genesis 4:15), Noah's rainbow sign (Genesis 9:12–17), the Passover blood and meal (Exodus 12:13; 13:9). The same Hebrew word translated 'sign' or 'mark' is used in each instance here. Note: The *sign and seal* given to the New Covenant beneficiaries is *the presence of God's Spirit* in their lives (Romans 8:16; Ephesians 1:13). While some suggest that 'love for one another' is the ultimate sign of the Christian (John 13:35 NKJV), such love is simply one aspect of the 'fruit' of the indwelling Spirit (Galatians 5:22). Ultimately, the presence of the Spirit is the evidence and sign of a true believer, manifesting Himself in many and varied ways.

4.    While male circumcision initially served a very practical purpose as a sign of remembrance for God's covenant people, the apostolic age would eventually reveal a profound *prophetic* purpose. For believers in Christ, both male and female, a 'circumcision of the heart' would occur, where Jesus Himself would remove the fleshly, sinful nature from those who would receive Him as Lord (Romans 2:29; Colossians 2:11–14).

5.    Genesis 12:10–17; 20:1–18; 24:1.

6.    Genesis 26:7–14.

7.    Genesis 27:19–36; 30:27–43; 31:19–42.

8.    Genesis 34:13–29; 35:22; 37:19–35; 38:12–25.

9. The *only men* in Abraham's line recorded as receiving or being threatened with God's judgment prior to Mt Sinai, were Judah's sons Er and Onan (Genesis 38:6–10), and Moses' son Gershom (Exodus 4:24–26). Besides this, the *one unique thing they have in common* is that each of these men were mothered by foreign women and were born and raised outside of the Israelite community. My suggestion is that these three men were therefore not circumcised at birth (certainly Gershom was not) and were not made aware of God's covenant with their forefather or of what it meant to 'walk before' Him (Genesis 17:1). They were therefore considered 'cut off' from Abraham's line (Genesis 17:14).

## Chapter 2: Israel 'under' Abraham

1. Exodus 2:24–25; 3:6–10, 21–22; 12:36; Psalm 105:37.

2. Exodus 11:4–7; 12:12–27; 13:6–10. Prior to this, God had sent a series of nine devastations on Egypt, and in the process makes 'a distinction' between His people and the Egyptians, as time and time again the Israelites remain *untouched* by these plagues (see Exodus 8:20–24; 9:1–7, 22–26; 10:21–23). The point is, the Lord knew very well who His people were. God Himself had no need of an external sign to reveal where His people lived. The Passover lamb's blood was not for *His* benefit—it was a sign for the sake of the Israelites (Exodus 12:13).

3. Two things worth noting on this point. Firstly, the blood shed by the Passover lamb was not the blood of the Old Covenant. The Mosaic Law Covenant, together with its blood and atoning sacrifices, was introduced at Mount Sinai months after Israel's escape from Egypt (Exodus 24:3–7; Hebrews 9:16–22). Secondly, the Exodus account of Passover does not itself relate the *ridding of yeast* to the *ridding of sinfulness*, as some suggest. True, the New Testament uses 'yeast' as an allegory for hypocrisy (Matthew 16:12; Luke 12:1; 1 Corinthians 5:6–8; Galatians 5:7–10), but not for sin or immorality in general.

4. Exodus 14:10–12, 21–31.

5. Exodus 15:22–25.

6. Exodus 16:1–36. It seems that no sooner were God's basic instructions given—to rest on the Sabbath and to not store the daily portion of manna overnight—than they were ignored. Clearly

the disobedience of God's people produced nothing good or lasting but resulted in rot and stench. However, the consequence of their waywardness was not God *punishing* them (as He does many times post-Sinai) but rather a *natural* repercussion of attempting to defy divine order.

7.   Exodus 17:1–7.

## Chapter 3: The Law-Keeping Covenant

# Together with the aged prophetess Anna, Simeon represents the last genuine prophetic voice to operate under the Old Covenant, prior to the preaching of Jesus' cousin John. See Luke 2:25–38.

1.   See also Deuteronomy 9:9–11; Hebrews 9:4.

2.   Exodus 32:7–10. It would appear the reason the Israelites (under Aaron's leadership) could so readily create and worship a golden calf, was due to their experiences in Egypt. Joshua 24:14 indicates that the Israelites worshipped the false gods of Egypt prior to the Exodus. Only now, under the Law Covenant and after Yahweh's *explicitly expressed desire* for a monotheistic nation, such worship was considered sinful (a violation of God's covenant) and therefore punishable by death.

3.   Deuteronomy 9:7–8, 18–20.

4.   Although God initially threatened to destroy the *entire* Israelite population for this act of idolatry (with the exception of Moses), He famously 'relents' in response to Moses' appeal—an appeal based on God's promised faithfulness to Abraham. You see, although the Law Covenant had just been introduced, it did not set aside, replace, or nullify the Abrahamic Covenant, but rather, served as an alternative agreement. These two covenants co-existed simultaneously, until Christ. See Luke 13:10–17; Galatians 3:15–17.

5.   Exodus 34–Numbers 10.

6.   Numbers 16:1–3, 31–35, 41–49.

7.   See for example, Deuteronomy 31:24–32, 35; Joshua 23:15–16; Jeremiah 3:8; 4:18–22; 15:5–9; 44:2–6.

8.   Luke 1:26–36; 2:8–15.

**Chapter 4: Out with the Old… in with the New**

1. See also Isaiah 40:3; Malachi 4:5–6; Matthew 3:1–12.

2. Not only is this one of the *first* titles given to Jesus in our New Testament, but in John's Revelation of Jesus Christ—the last book of the Bible—Jesus is referred to as *the Lamb* more than any other designation: some thirty times in those twenty-two final chapters.

3. Luke 22:7–20; 1 Corinthians 11:23–26.

4. Isaiah 53:12; Luke 22:37; Hebrews 9:15; 1 Peter 3:18.

5. See also Romans 11:26–27; Hebrews 10:1–18.

6. See also Luke 3:16; Acts 2:32–33.

7. See also, from Jesus, Matthew 4:17 (ESV).

8. John 1:14; 14:9; 17:4–6; Colossians 1:15; Hebrews 1:3.

9. See also John 19:38–42; 20:1–29; Acts 1:9–11; 2:32–33; 1 Corinthians 15:3–8; Hebrews 1:3; 8:1–2; 9:23–28; 10:12.

10. Matthew 27:48–51; John 19:29–30.

11. Romans 10:4; Hebrews 2:2; 8:7–13; 10:9. While it's clear that the completion of the Old Covenant was *announced* by Christ at Calvary, there is a case to be made that its end was not *actualised* until the Temple was destroyed forty years later. Although a detailed analysis of this view is beyond the scope of this book, consider the accounts of brothers Ishmael and Isaac (representing a covenant transition), and Kings Saul and David (a kingdom transition). Both demonstrate a notable period of time between the *arrival* of the new and the *removal* of the old, during which the old order persecutes the new.

12. It is my understanding that the Law Covenant was inaugurated at Sinai on the fiftieth day—after seven completed weeks—following the sprinkling of covenant blood (Exodus 24:3–18; 32:15–28). That day, 3,000 people were cut down by the swords of their Levite brothers as a result of 'the ministry that brought death'. In direct contrast, on the fiftieth day after the shedding of Christ's blood (the Day of Pentecost), the Holy Spirit was poured out on God's newly formed covenant nation—the Church—a new order of priesthood was established, and, as a result of being 'cut to the heart' by the preaching of Peter, *3,000 people were saved* that day by 'the ministry that brings [God's gift of] righteousness'. Acts 2:1–41; 2 Corinthians 3:6–9; 1 Peter 2:4–5; Revelation 1:4–6; 5:9–10.

13. Romans 3:20–24. It is worth noting that in Philippians 3:3–9 (quoted in full at the conclusion of the *Final Thoughts* Chapter), Paul describes 'confidence in the flesh' (Greek: *sarx*) as exercising confidence in one's *pedigree and/or performance,* a value he subsequently considers 'rubbish' in light of his newly found *position* in Christ.

## Chapter 5: The New Covenant

1. John 1:14, 18; 1 John 4:9.
2. John 20:17; Hebrews 2:11–12.
3. John 1:12; Romans 8:17; Galatians 4:5.
4. Galatians 3:16.
5. Genesis 22:18; Romans 4:13; Galatians 3:6–8.
6. Galatians 3:14, 26–29.
7. Genesis 12:2–3; 15:1–7; 17:1–8; Romans 4:16–17; Galatians 3:7–9.
8. Hebrews 4:15; 1 Peter 1:19.
9. See also Isaiah 53:9.
10. Hebrews 9:26–28; 10:10–14.
11. It is widely known that Deuteronomy 28 is dedicated entirely to listing specific examples of the blessings and curses promised under the Law Covenant. However, of the sixty-eight verses in that chapter, only thirteen—less than 20%—speak of the blessings. The overwhelming emphasis of that passage is placed on the covenant curses, of which 'Christ redeemed us' (Galatians 3:10–14).
12. See also Deuteronomy 5:33; 7:11–15; 26:16–19; 30:9; 32:9.
13. Jeremiah 31:31–34; Romans 4:5–8; Hebrews 10:17.
14. Ezekiel 37:26–28; Acts 15:5–8.

## Conclusion: God Qualifies You!

1. Hebrews 8:6–13; 10:9.
2. Galatians 3:1.
3. See also 1 Timothy 1:7–11.
4. Galatians 1:6–7; 2:14–16; 6:12–16.

**Final Thoughts: The Progression of God's Covenants**

1.  Genesis 6:5–13.

2.  Genesis 18:16–19:29; Ezekiel 16:49–50.

3.  See, for example, 1 Thessalonians 4:1–12; 1 Timothy 3:14–15; Titus 2:1–3; 1 Peter 3:1–16.

4.  Proverbs 22:15; 23:13–14; 29:15.

5.  This distinction of covenant identities, between 'child' and 'son', is somewhat reminiscent of the account of Abraham's two boys, Ishmael and Isaac. When God refers to Ishmael, He speaks of him as a 'boy' (Hebrew: *na'ar*), but describes Isaac, the younger brother, as Abraham's 'son' (Hebrew: *bên*). Paul explains how these two brothers serve as a metaphor for the people of the Old Covenant—represented by Ishmael—and those of the New Covenant—the 'children of promise'. A similar (albeit a more subtle) comparison of this, occurs in Jesus' Parable of the Kissing Father. In that story, the father refers to the younger brother as 'this *son* [Greek: *huios*] of mine', whereas he opts to refer to the older brother using the word *teknon*... a term most often translated as '*child*'. Again, the humbled and grateful recipient of grace is called '*son*', whereas the self-righteous brother—clearly a reference to the legalistic Jews—is called '*child*'. See Genesis 21:12–20; 22:2, 16; Luke 15:24, 31; Galatians 4:22–31.

6.  The word translated 'guardian' in this text—sometimes rendered 'schoolmaster' or 'tutor'—is the Greek word *paidagōgos*, from which comes the English derivative 'pedagogue'.

7.  Matthew 10:1; 28:18–20; Galatians 3:7–9, 14.

8.  See also Matthew 28:19–20; John 17:18.

9.  John 8:29; 1 Corinthians 6:20; 2 Corinthians 1:20; 5:9; Colossians 1:10; 1 Timothy 2:3.

10. See also John 17:18; 2 Corinthians 5:20.

11. Jeremiah 31:33; Ezekiel 36:26–27; Hebrews 10:16.

12. See also Romans 8:15–16; 1 John 2:27.

# SCRIPTURE INDEX

# ABOUT THE AUTHOR

**www.chadmansbridge.com**

Husband to Jaye and father to four amazing kids, Chad M. Mansbridge is also a pastor, author, content creator, conference speaker, and one of Australia's most dynamic Bible teachers, known for his ability to communicate profound and complex truth with clarity, simplicity, and a whole lot of fun! At twenty-three years of age, Chad and Jaye pioneered Bayside Church International, a thriving local church on the south coast of South Australia.

A loveable Aussie larrikin with an infectious zest for life, Chad carries an unshakable desire to see people walk in an authentic and unhindered relationship with their Maker, and is regularly invited to speak at churches, colleges, and conference events throughout Australia and overseas.

Follow Chad on your favourite social media platform: @Chad.M.Mansbridge

Made in United States
Orlando, FL
03 November 2022

24172882R00039